CHRISTIANITY
for NON-CHRISTIANS

(WHAT DO CHRISTIANS BELIEVE?)

D1565513

GREG GILLHAM

ISBN 978-1-64300-569-0 (Paperback)
ISBN 978-1-64300-570-6 (Digital)

Covenant Books, Inc.
11661 Hwy 707
Murrells Inlet, SC 29576
www.covenantbooks.com

CONTENTS

FOREWORD

In life, many decisions offer multiple choices—should we have pizza, burgers, or Chinese for supper? Which college do I attend? Some decisions, however, are between only two choices. This book discusses one of those decisions, namely—will you choose to be a Christian or not. Everyone is born into this world as a non-Christian; and it requires a conscious decision to become a Christian.

It is my intention, as a Christian, to present some introduction to a Christian worldview and to discuss some basics of Christianity. There is a great deal of false information about and bias against Christianity, which creates apprehension in those who have had no exposure to it. By reading this book, I applaud your curiosity and desire to know more. If you are a Christian, I hope you find encouragement in these pages. If you are not Christian, chances are you know one.

As a non-Christian, you may wonder what about that person makes them a Christian. After all, you have many things in common with them including hobbies, food preferences, political views and interest in travel, among dozens of other things.

What you may not realize is—what makes your Christian friend different from you has to do with their understanding of who we are as people, why we are here, how we make life choices, and what do we consider to be true in life.

There are innumerable "truths" in the world— the sky appears blue, puppies are cute, and I can't dunk a basketball. The truth we are pursuing in this book concerns faith and religious belief. Many people mistakenly believe that each person must find their own truth and follow it. One real truth is— not all religions are true and most are leading people down a (spiritually) dead end road. How can I say that? Consider this—the various "truths" of the major religions directly contradict the "truths" of the other major religions.

For instance, the following are brief superficial summaries of some major religions. Christians believe in one God and that Jesus Christ was God in

CHRISTIANITY FOR NON-CHRISTIANS

human form who lived on earth, died for our sins, and was resurrected from the dead. Muslims believe Jesus was a great prophet; but they believe he was neither God, crucified, nor resurrected. Judaism believes in the Christian God but denies that Jesus was God. Buddhism largely rejects the concept of God and believes that life involves suffering and that suffering may be avoided with meditation and right thinking. Hindus may believe in many gods and some believe that everything is god. Atheism lacks belief in any god; and therefore is not considered to be a religion by many.

These are the world's major religions and as you can see, they are a bit conflicting. Thus, it should be apparent that not all religions can be true. They can all be wrong; but they can't all be right.

It will be impossible to find truth if one is looking in the wrong place. Finding truth involves several steps, including: 1) acknowledgement of truth's existence; 2) curiosity to pursue it; 3) expending effort to find and recognize it; 4) thinking about it carefully; 5) testing it in light of other known truths; 6) deciding to accept (or reject) it; 7) internalizing it; and finally, 8) begin living it. This seems like several steps but it is a logical progression of how most people would pursue something of importance.

FOREWORD

Simply by reading this book, you will have taken the first three steps on your path to finding truth. To know truth is to say that there must be an entity that decides what truth is. After all, truth isn't up for a vote. *Truth just is.* We therefore must begin with the Truth Giver, God.

GOD

Before we can discover who God is, we have to consider whether God exists. Unfortunately there are some who believe that no god exists. Others believe that a god exists, but is indifferent to us. The Christian God is one who desperately wants us to know that he exists and wants a relationship with us. He has revealed himself to us through the Bible and the world around us.

In **Exodus 3:14** of the Bible, Moses is asking God for his name. God responds, "I am who I am." In essence, God states that he just *is*. He exists eternally—he has no beginning or end. All things in our world have a beginning, which means there is something that caused that thing to exist. This is cause and effect—meaning that for every outcome (effect), there is a cause. God is the great effect without a cause. He is eternal past, present, and eternal future. He existed before time or space. In fact, he created time and space.

Consider nature, its laws of gravity and physics, the stars, atoms within a molecule, and the complexity within a single cell bacterium. The bacterium has 1) DNA; 2) an outside cell wall to keep harmful things out and useful things in; 3) the ability to determine which is useful or harmful; 4) the ability to take in the useful things; 5) a means to use them to produce proteins crucial for life maintenance; 6) a process to produce energy; 7) the ability to reproduce; 8) the means to dispose of waste and toxins; and perhaps 9) the ability to move within its environment, to name a few.

That is just in a single cell bacterium. Do you believe this is all an accident? Consider Darwinism and the theory of evolution. Darwin had no explanation for how life originated. How does it accidently happen that *nonliving* atoms join to form a molecule, which then joins other molecules to form a compound. This compound (without the ability to move) must then randomly, accidently, join other "like" compounds in an appropriate environment, with all the necessary circumstances, in just an exact manner to result in tissue capable of life—namely surviving, thriving, and, ultimately, reproducing.

Living tissue from nonliving atoms? If you placed rocks, soil, water, oxygen, carbon, light, pressure, heat, and a hundred other elements in an open space and waited a million years, do you think life would evolve from that? This is Darwin's theory of evolution; and it is a foundational belief of many who don't believe in a living God who created life. Darwinism is a shortcut to atheism, which asserts that non-life produced, or mutated into, life. If life can spontaneously sprout from the nonliving, a God isn't necessary. This is what some people prefer because they don't like the rules that come with a God.

Regardless of how much evidence exists for God and the lack of evidence proving life arose from non-life, an argument or debate isn't going to convince anyone that a God exists. That requires faith to believe in the evidence that God has provided for us.

God reveals enough evidence for his existence such that he can be found by those desiring a relationship with him. However, he will not be so obvious, such that, those who do not pursue him will not find him.

So who is God? God says, "I am the First and I am the Last. Besides me, there is no God" (**Isaiah 44:6**).

God is a *trinity*—meaning there is God, the Father in heaven (I don't know where that is!), Jesus Christ (God in human form), and the Holy Spirit—which is God sent to dwell inside the hearts of Christians.

The concept of the Trinity is quite difficult for Christians to grasp since we have nothing in our physical world similar to this. However, just because it is difficult to grasp doesn't make it impossible or untrue. Does anyone know how the human mind works? Yet, it is there and we are all aware of it. Do you want a God you can completely understand and explain?

God tells us about himself in the Bible. The very first of his Ten Commandments is "Thou shalt have no other gods before me." This means he is a jealous God and we are to follow him alone. You may notice I refer to God as "He." Jesus, in the Bible, teaches us how to pray with the Lord's Prayer. It begins with "Our Father, who art in heaven …" Thus God is identified with male attributes. (As an aside, many people use this to justify a belief that men are supe-rior to women. That is absolutely false. While the Bible may identify the male as spiritual leader of the home, it also states husband and wife must submit to each other. Many women played prominent roles in the Bible.) In addition to being a jealous God, he also demonstrates:

1) His *Omnipotence* (all powerful nature). Nothing happens in the universe without God's allowing or causing it. Notice he *allows* some things which he may not have caused. This means that bad or harmful events are possible, even though God doesn't cause them. Because he is all powerful, that makes God sovereign, i.e. the boss.

2) His *Omniscience* (all knowing). He knows how many cells are in your body and how many grains of sand on the beaches of the Caribbean. He knows all future events and actions; *but* that doesn't mean he influences our decision-making or causes us to act in a certain manner. He simply knows the future. He also knows what is good and good for us. We may not understand many things, such as evil or suffering, but he knows the part they play in the present and future.

3) His *Omni benevolence* (all good). God created the universe and all living things. He loves it all and desires only good for his cre-

ation. He knows when a greater good will result from, what appears to us to be, a very bad event or situation.

4) His *Righteousness* (sinless). God is without sin and cannot be in its presence, or the presence of evil. God just doesn't decide what is righteous, he is righteous. He is the prototype of being sinless.

5) God is also *Just* (fair and consistent), *Intelligent* (his universe has order and is governed by natural laws such as mathematics, chemistry, etc.), *Unchanging* (he is perfect, doesn't need to alter himself through time and doesn't require updates like our phone apps!).

6) God's attribute of *Love* certainly deserves discussion since God is most assuredly a God of love. God's love is unconditional and is a never ending desire for us to be in communion with him. He wants what is best for us—fellowship with him and other Christians. He wants us to be happy, healthy, content, and free from worry or doubts. He created us to be loved by him and for us to love him. It's important to note that love cannot be coerced or forced.

A person can threaten another and force them to say 'I love you;' but that doesn't mean the feeling is there. Love is a decision. We have to choose to love God.

To have this choice means we are free and able to choose. Therefore, God is also a God of *Freedom*. He wants our love and gave us the choice to love him. It is his desire that all of us would love him and be with him for eternity. He could never force us to love him, because it wouldn't be love.

Genesis 1:1 begins with "In the beginning, God created the …" In summary, God is your Creator and he loves you. He loves us enough to come to earth in person and show us how to love and live. That person is Jesus Christ.

JESUS

Jesus Christ was a real person and is a part of the Trinity. He was a man of Jewish decent who is found in non-Christian historical documents and his existence is widely accepted among historians and academics. Jesus was born of a woman, ate food, required sleep, experienced human emotions, and ultimately died a physical death. Many skeptics say he was just a man—a philosopher or prophet.

Christians believe him to have been God in human flesh. By this it is meant that God took human form and walked among us on this earth. By taking human form, he was subject to the physical limitations of the human body. As an infant, he required feeding, cleaning, and protection. As a youth, he worked with his earthly father, Joseph, who was a carpenter. He studied the Jewish faith and as his knowledge grew, he realized that he was sent to earth for a very specific purpose.

Luke 2:39-52 is a very brief summary of his early years. As he gained understanding of who he was, he grew in wisdom. He learned the history of Israel and the writings of the Old Testament prophets who came before him. Knowing the scriptures, he realized he was the fulfillment of the Old Testament prophesies and the covenant God had made with Israel and mankind.

When he had grown to a man of thirty years, he was baptized and began his earthly ministry. You may wonder who would be qualified to baptize God's son. That was John the Baptist who was specifically sent by God to foretell of Jesus's birth and appearance on earth (**John 1:6–8**).

Jesus was a patient, kind, and thoughtful teacher of the people of Israel and anyone who would listen. He taught about who God is and the meaning of the Old Testament writings in effort to bring people to knowledge of God's plan for them. He often spoke in parables rather than formal teaching or a lecture.

Through prayer and living a sinless life, the power and blessing of performing miracles was realized. He demonstrated compassion and empathy by healing the sick and raising the dead. He sat and ate with the outcasts of that time, namely tax collectors, lepers, and prostitutes. He came for everyone. By commanding the winds to halt and changing water to wine, he demonstrated power over nature. It was this power and his growing popularity which was a threat to the leaders of Israel, namely the Pharisees and Sadducees. They worried he would replace them as ruler because his following was growing as was his fame.

Jesus was intelligent and able to debate with the Jewish leaders and demonstrated to the Jews how ungodly their leaders were. Because of the threat to their power, the Pharisees and Sadducees devised a plan to remove him from their society.

This is the homestretch of the mission Jesus was ultimately sent to accomplish. The nation Israel was under control of the Roman Empire at the time of Jesus's life. The Jewish leaders lied to the Romans that Jesus was creating disturbances among the Jews to rise up against the Romans. When the Romans found no evidence of this, they asked the Jews what they wanted the Romans to do with Jesus. By the end of the trial, the Jewish leaders had turned the Jews against Jesus and convinced the Jews to request crucifixion for Jesus. Crucifixion was a common form of Roman execution at that time.

In the Old Testament, prior to Jesus's appearance on earth, God required frequent animal blood sacrifices for *temporary* payment of sin. The animals were innocent of sin and were a foreshadowing of God's future plan for payment of sin. Thus, forgiveness of sin has always required blood (**Hebrews 9:22**). It is a symbol of death (sin) and dying to an old "sinful" self to allow a new "forgiven" self. Jesus knew his ultimate mission was to die on the cross. In fact, he predicted it in **Matthew 17:22–23**.

Jesus, being innocent (like the animal sacrifices), was God's plan to be the *permanent* payment for sin. Jesus, who was God in flesh, could have used his heavenly power to avoid the painful death; but instead, he willingly allowed himself to be crucified. Jesus did more than predict his crucifixion however. As in **Matthew 17:23**, Jesus in **John 16:16–22,** predicts what would occur after his death—his resurrection from the grave three days later. This resurrection miracle was the symbol of Jesus's triumph over sin and death. It also represents the new "forgiven" self which results after the death of one's old "sinful" self.

Jesus was witnessed by hundreds of people in the days after the resurrection (**1 Corinthians 15:3-8**). He still had the nail marks on his wrists and feet and the spear piercings on his side (**John 20:24-29**). It is because of these eye witness accounts that people began converting to Christianity—they had witnessed its God, in flesh, as well as the hope, love, forgiveness, and grace offered by him to all who would receive it.

Not long after his resurrection, Jesus was seen being taken into heaven (**Acts 1:8-11**). Prior to his ascension into heaven, Jesus commanded the disciples, and all future Christians, to tell everyone that he died for all who would accept him as savior (the payment for their sin) (**Luke 24:46–48**).

Prior to his death, Jesus said he was the *only* way to heaven (**John 14:6**). Many do not like this Christian belief because they think it makes Christians "intolerant" of other religions. Christians don't independently decide to believe that--Jesus himself told the world he is the only way to heaven. It is a teaching of the Bible, which, as we will see, is given to us by God.

When Jesus ascended into heaven, his followers were frightened they would be left alone and without their God. God had a plan for that too. After the ascension, the disciples and all believers soon had God in their presence again, when God sent the Holy Spirit.

THE HOLY SPIRIT

T he Holy Spirit is the third portion of the Trinity. It was sent by God to dwell in the hearts of those who desire a relationship with God and who accept Jesus as their savior from their sin (**Acts 2:1–4**). Everyone has a ruler of their heart—the only two choices are the Holy Spirit or Satan. The Holy Spirit can be likened to God's voice within the Christian and the captain of our spiritual ship. When Christians are in fellowship with God, we are constantly listening to the Holy Spirit which acts as the ruler of our heart and mind.

When the Holy Spirit is the ruler of the Christian heart, that means Satan is no longer welcome. The Spirit prompts the Christian to pray and reminds us to avoid profanity and the spreading of gossip. It influences us to view events from a heavenly perspective, to be thankful for all that God has done and to count our blessings. It should guide our spiritual decision-making and lead us to emulate Christ.

The Holy Spirit warns us when we are dangerously close to sinful behavior and convicts us when we have sinned. It is different than a conscience. The conscience is the knowledge of right and wrong placed on everyone's heart by God. Everyone has a conscience even though not everyone is a Christian. Not everyone listens to their conscience as evidenced by the evening news. The Christian, when walking in fellowship with God, is in frequent contact with the Holy Spirit within them and may have an ongoing internal dialog with it throughout the day.

I mentioned a Christian who is in fellowship with God. Not all Christians are in fellowship with God at all times. Christians can struggle with their faith in times of illness, financial stress, loss of a loved one, or during a period of doubt concerning their faith. We can have periods of pride when we ignore the Holy Spirit and follow our own selfish desires. We can feel hopeless or discouraged and have sinful tendencies just like non-Christians.

When out of fellowship with God, a Christian may not feel the presence of the Holy Spirit and even ignore the Spirit's prompting to behave in a manner worthy of Jesus's name. This can lead to a life which appears inconsistent with Christian faith. These (brief) periods of time may indicate great internal struggle for that Christian.

Once a Christian has felt the love, closeness, and fellowship in a relationship with God, it can be a period of loneliness and hopelessness if God has distanced himself from the Christian. It is a period of gentle discipline by God to nudge us back towards him and to resume living a life worthy of Jesus's name.

EVIL AND SIN

I have mentioned sin on a few occasions and it must be defined and discussed a bit. Sin is thinking or behaving in a manner inconsistent with God's commandments or against his will. Sin had its beginnings very early after God created the heavens and earth.

As mentioned above, God allows us freedom to choose whether we will follow him or not. By giving us the freedom to choose, we can choose to *act*, or *act otherwise.* Some of God's early creations were the angels, who also had the freedom to choose. The significance of this freedom of choice means that when choices are made, consequences follow.

One of the angels, Lucifer (aka Satan, the Devil), chose to not worship God, and thus evil was born. Satan is the author of evil and his first sin was one of pride when he chose to not worship God. He was banished from heaven because God cannot be in the presence of evil or sin. It is important to clarify that God did not create sin or evil. He did however create the *possibility* of sin and evil by giving the angels (and us) the freedom of choice.

Satan is as real as the air we breathe—do not doubt that. Since his creation, Satan has been at war with God for dominion over all of creation, especially us. Satan is battling to take as many of us as possible with him into his eternity. He knows he has already lost the war. Christ won the war over sin and death by rising from the grave.

Because he is so evil and depraved, Satan's goal is to create as much pain and suffering as possible. Satan realizes that the best way to hurt God is to separate God from us, his beloved creations.

After Adam and Eve were created, God gave them the Garden of Eden and one rule—don't eat the apples from the Tree of Knowledge. That is when the potential for human sin was created. Adam and Eve were given one rule and the choice to obey it or not. Satan was there to tempt them to eat the apples. They chose to eat the apple when Satan told them they would be like God and know what God knows. Thus sin was born in all subsequent human beings and sin's father is Satan.

Sin takes all forms. There are sins of commission (our actions) and sins of omission (not doing things we should). Our thoughts are a deadly breeding ground for sin because there is no outwardly evidence of a sinful thought, unless it gives birth to a sinful deed. Likewise, sin in the privacy of our own home or when we are alone is dangerous because no one else sees it and the sin goes without confrontation.

One fact which is easily forgotten (or ignored) is that God is constantly aware of our thoughts and actions. Thus our sin is always seen by the One who has forbidden it. We all have our individual weaknesses and temptations, which are more difficult to resist than others. Sin results from our thoughts or actions, which overflow from what is in our hearts. A heart ruled by the Holy Spirit more easily resists temptation than a heart ruled by Satan.

As a result of sin entering the world, the perfect paradise of the Garden of Eden disappeared from our lives and the consequences of sin appeared. The consequences include pain, suffering, illness, hunger, death, loneliness, hopelessness, and innumerable others.

Sin can be difficult to recognize if a person lives in a culture overflowing with sin. Attitudes or actions which are acceptable in a society may still be contrary to God's commands and are thus sinful. Greed, lust, intoxication, premarital sex, selfishness, and pursuit of power are all common examples in our American society.

This vast chasm between a culture's acceptable behavior and God's commandments places Christians in a precarious situation in the culture. A Christian, adhering to God's law, may be labeled as intolerant or judgmental when we choose not to accept or participate in a culture's accepted sinful behaviors or attitudes. We are merely following God's instructions. They are the Ten Commandments, not suggestions.

It is important to understand God's expectations for us and know his commandments. They are recorded in the Bible which is where we must go next.

THE BIBLE

The Bible is the Christian roadmap to God in heaven. Before we reach heaven, it is the instruction manual for Christian beliefs, actions, attitudes, and worldview while we are on earth. It is an incredible book and most people (many Christians included) do not appreciate the wisdom and timeless truths on its pages.

Although written by humans, it is God-inspired (**2 Timothy 3:16-17**) and written by over forty authors spanning many centuries. We already know how the Holy Spirit can inhabit our hearts and influence our thoughts and actions. Therefore, it isn't difficult to grasp that God, four thousand years ago, could inspire prophets to write scripture (the Old Testament) about Christ before he was born. Likewise, two thousand years ago, God used Christ's disciples to record his teachings which have become the New Testament.

The Bible consists of the Old and New Testaments. Although written over many centuries by different authors, its meaning and message are consistent from beginning to end. The life of Christ separates them in time, the Old Testament recorded before and the New Testament recorded after his life. The two Testaments were not written as Testaments. They are a coalition of hand-written manuscripts which had been found. Many manuscripts had been found but not all were included in the Bible.

What was to be included was decided by (again, God inspired and approved) Jewish historians and scholars who were familiar with the culture and events at the time the manuscripts were written. This is how God preserved a true and accurate Bible—his word to us.

The Old Testament tells the story of how the Jewish people came to exist after creation and how God led them out of slavery (in Egypt) to a land he promised to them, Israel. He used many prophets over many centuries to tell Israel of his plan and not to stray from him.

Israel strayed many times and often followed false gods or foreign gods. God used prophets to warn Israel to reject the false gods and sinful lifestyles. The prophets predicted severe future consequences if Israel didn't respond; and they also predicted God's blessing if Israel did respond. These predictions are called prophesy.

The New Testament is God's new covenant, or promise, with mankind. It references Old Testament prophesies fulfilled by Jesus's appearance and ministry. Many prophesies, written centuries before Christ's birth, foretold the arrival of a savior for Israel and all mankind. The prophesies detailed how this would occur, who it would be, the manner of his arrival, his ministry, how he would be accepted, how he would then be rejected, how he would be crucified, and ultimately how he would rise from death. Therefore, Jesus's life and death were prophesied, with incredible detail and accuracy, centuries before he arrived.

The prophesied events of Christ's life are so numerous, so detailed, and predict such highly unlikely events, that it can only be concluded that God inspired the writings. We saw previously how God knows the future; and by predicting the future through prophetic writings, God reveals himself to us.

In addition to prophesy, the Bible also contains history; and the first four books of the New

Testament, called Gospels, are good examples of this history. The Gospels record Jesus's teachings and miracles, which are historical events. Because they are written by disciples who traveled with Jesus and witnessed his life and miracles, the Gospels can be viewed as reliable and accurate.

In addition to history, the Bible contains poetry, encouragement, comfort, commandments, promises, and timeless wisdom. It gives us guidelines on how to find a spouse, raise children, how to manage our money, and confront sin. It also demonstrates how to be a blessing to others, how to love, how to recognize evil, and how to heal relationships.

Many like to discredit the Bible citing what they believe to be inconsistencies on its pages. Centuries ago, when original Old Testament manuscripts were written, they were copied and shared through-out Israel. Likewise, New Testament manuscripts recorded by Christ's followers were hand-copied and distributed to the new Christians throughout the Roman Empire and surrounding geographical areas.

The inconsistencies cited by skeptics are those errors, human errors, which occurred by copying the manuscripts. If we asked twenty people to go see a movie and write a summary of it, they would be similar but not identical. Certain events would impact people differently.

Likewise, if we asked twenty people to copy ten pages of a dictionary, do you think there would be some errors? Of course there would be; *but* they would be different mistakes on different pages! That is what minimizes the significance of the errors—they are sporadic and random. This doesn't affect the validity of the text. The copies carry a similar interpretation which yields doctrinal consistency.

It is noteworthy that not all people accept the Bible as God-inspired. There are those who believe it to be more of a historical document which only applies to the past. These differences of interpretation have led to divisions between various Christians, which have given birth to different Christian denominations.

This view of the Bible leads to two broad categories in Christian theology and doctrine. Those who view the Bible as God-inspired and timeless are the more conservative Christian denominations. They believe the Bible is perfect and requires no updating or changes for our contemporary lives. The more liberal denominations believe the Bible to be more specific to Israel's early history and thus is open to interpretation in our time.

These differences, which are monumental, have led to a great many denominations who all consider themselves as Christian. It is because of the differences in biblical interpretation that there are denominations who disagree about gay marriage, how to baptize new Christians, who can take communion, which day is the Sabbath, and scores of other topics.

It is understandable how non-Christians can be confused about what represents a true Christian faith. A Christianity adhering to different biblical interpretations leads to Christians believing contradictory doctrines, which results in contradictory behavior. This gives the appearance of hypocrisy which devastates the reputation of Christianity.

So who is right?

It must always come down to truth. We know humans are innately sinful and therefore predisposed to misinterpret the Bible. We will have a tendency to interpret it in a way favorable to our worldview. Many people reject the Bible because it places restrictions on our thoughts and behavior, which makes people feel judged. For most people, it is easier to reject the Bible than it is to change behavior or thinking.

Being a subscriber to the conservative view of the Bible, I accept and follow the Bible as written. If we accept that it is God-inspired, and God wants to reveal himself to us through the Bible, and God doesn't make errors, and God is all powerful, then God certainly would be able to ensure his word, the Bible, is exactly as he desires it.

The Bible is God's book given to us to be followed while on this earth. So, what happens after we die? In a word: Eternity.

ETERNITY

The word eternity is known by most people. Grasping its meaning as a mortal is challenging since we really only have knowledge of finite things in our world. We view eternity as a future that is infinitely far away; but eternity also includes the infinite past. While God is eternal, past and future, we are not. God knew he was going to create us in eternity past but our physical existence began when we were conceived.

In the Christian faith, eternity future is significant because it marks the beginning of our spiritual existence after physical death. We can be sure we have an eternal existence. As mortals, it's not natural for us to pursue or welcome death. By nature, we have the desire and instinct to survive. God made us that way. We are hard-wired for eternity.

I fear many people who believe there is no God just presume that they will cease to exist after they die. It will be "lights out," just like turning off the switch. They think they will have no awareness of anything. As a Christian, I know they became eternal spiritual beings the moment they were created. I believe if non-Christians understood that, they would more strongly consider their beliefs and eternities. Some think they will be reincarnated after death. Reincarnation is inconsistent with Christianity.

The Bible gives us an idea of what eternity will be like. Jesus tells a parable in **Luke 16:19-31**. In it, a man dies and goes to a place of torment because he refused God in his lifetime. In the parable, the man requests that Abraham (in heaven) please dip his finger in water and quench the man's thirst. He also asks Abraham to warn the man's brothers that this place of torment really does exist.

This parable tells us several things. It tells us the man feels thirst and torment, therefore he is aware of how he feels. He is capable of speaking to Abraham and can also hear his response. He recalls his brothers, therefore he has memory of his time on earth.

In the parable, Abraham tells the man of an impassable chasm between the place of torment and heaven. The place of torment is what we consider hell.

Hell is described in many ways in the Bible—one of which is a burning hot, never-ending fire pit. It has been described that way to relate the misery, hopelessness, depravity, loneliness, and unhappiness that results when we are separated from God. In **Matthew 11:20–24**, Jesus states there will be varying degrees of punishment for those in hell, in accordance with their deeds on earth. This is also recorded in **Revelation 20:11-13**.

Hell is reserved specifically for those who choose to reject a relationship with God. Many wonder how a loving God could allow a hell to exist. If we recall, God is a god of freedom and choice. Choices have consequences. People don't reject God because of a lack of evidence. There is enough evidence for God's existence as we discussed above. People reject God because of a refusal to admit they need a God. If they reject him on earth, why would he force them to be in his presence for eternity? Since he is a just God, there must be payment for sin and rejecting him.

Why aren't those people already miserable on earth if they reject God here? One reason is that God has Satan on a leash. Satan is free to do many evil things—but not all that he would like to do. God has a spiritual presence (Christians) on earth and also has his hand of restraint against the evil that Satan would perpetrate on the earth. A second reason non-Christians aren't miserable on earth is that while still on earth, they have time to find Jesus and become a believer. That is where Christians on earth have a role to play. Jesus commanded Christians to spread the good news that he came for anyone who would believe (**Matthew 28:18–20**).

The other place in eternity is heaven, where God is. I have no idea where that is and doubt I could comprehend it. Nevertheless, if God is there, that means there is no sin, temptation, doubt, pain, illness, hopelessness, or anger. When there, the purpose of believers will be to praise and love God and fellowship with other Christians. **Matthew 5:12** states that the rewards will be great in heaven.

I believe the phrase "eternal life" is confusing for many people. As mortal beings, we tend to view things in terms of physical life or death. When life is spoken of in the Bible, it frequently is referring to our spiritual life. We all have eternal "spiritual" lives—it's just a matter of whether we spend it in the presence of God or not.

Our physical life is very brief—the blink of an eye on the clock of eternity. Our spiritual lives are forever and that is what we should be focused on.

The Bible is clear—while we are mortals, we are to pursue God and godly lives. We have only until our physical death to make that decision. The Bible tells us that after our physical death, our eternal fate is sealed.

How can we possibly make it to heaven if we are all sinners? That is possible only because of God's grace.

GRACE

Grace is what makes it possible for us to be in heaven with God for eternity. We know God can't be in the presence of sin but he wants us to be with him. Since we mortals are innately sinful, we needed a way to remove our sin from us. Recall that Jesus offered himself as a sinless sacrifice on the cross to pay for our sins.

God didn't have to provide that payment. Because we have broken his commands countless times and ignored his callings, we don't deserve to be with God—and yet he provided a path to himself for us. That is grace. Grace is the giving of something good to someone who is undeserving of that good.

Like love, grace is something that can't be earned. We could never work hard enough or do enough good deeds to earn God's grace. He gives it unconditionally. We simply have to choose to accept it (**Ephesians 2:8–9**).

By offering us grace, God also demonstrates mercy towards us. Mercy is the withholding of something bad from someone who is deserving of that bad. By our sin, we deserve an eternity apart from God, which is very bad. Through his mercy, he offers us a way to avoid that. By his grace, he offers eternity with him even though we don't deserve it.

Besides forgiveness of our sins, we also receive God's blessing in our lives. Blessing may be something very pleasant such as a beautiful spring day or an opportunity to do God's will in our daily routine. It may be the ability to work at our job, offer comfort to someone, or the relief from suffering.

Believe it or not, suffering can actually be a blessing because it presents an opportunity to grow in faith which can be a Christian's testimony to non-Christians. We shouldn't complain when we experience suffering, although that is easier said than done. We forget that no matter how much difficulty or pain we are experiencing, it is only by God's mercy that it isn't worse!

As an aside, we also receive wisdom when we accept God's grace. He will grant us wisdom if we truly desire to become more like Christ. To achieve that requires prayer and Bible study. Wisdom is not exactly the same as knowledge. Knowledge is being aware of, or knowing, facts and details. Wisdom is knowledge applied with a Biblical worldview and some understanding of the Bible and who God is.

By receiving God's forgiveness through his grace, we are acknowledging we have sinned and also desire to avoid sin. Even though we desire to avoid it, we can't avoid sin all of the time; but that should now be our intention and desire. That desire to stop committing sin is called *repentance.*

Repentance is what turns our lives around when we become a Christian. We act and think differently. We view world events through the prism of God-given wisdom and see others as a body and eternal soul created by God. We look for opportunities to share Christ with those who would listen and to help those in physical or spiritual need. We want to be lights of hope in the world.

In short, after we have admitted sin, accepted God's grace and forgiveness, and repented by turning away from our sin, we have begun our journey down the path to become more like Jesus. Granted, we will never quite make it while here on earth—but what a fantastic goal! What if everyone had that as their goal? Imagine what the world would be like.

Sadly, becoming like Jesus is not the goal of most people, or even many people. It is safe to say, most people in this world are not Christians.

WHO IS (AND ISN'T)
A CHRISTIAN?

At first glance, this chapter title may appear quite judgmental. It isn't intended to be. The goal of this chapter is simply to help you, the reader, to understand whether or not you are a Christian.

It must be said at this time that only God knows what is in each person's heart and therefore only he knows who is or isn't a Christian. Could Hitler have had a last second change of heart and asked forgiveness before he died? Although it doesn't seem likely, only God knows.

All mortals, who have ever lived, will stand before God on judgment day and give an account of their lives and spiritual condition. We will be sent to heaven or hell based on if we have accepted Christ.

God will be the judge and, fortunately, he is perfect, fair, and just. There will be no bad or incorrect judgments made.

The Bible says "few" will be accepted in heaven. That means Christians. **Matthew 7:13–14** says that the path to heaven is narrow and few find it; while the path to destruction is wide.

If you are a Christian you have nothing to worry about. Here are some doctrinal basics which heaven-bound Christians believe:

1) Jesus was God who walked the earth;
2) Jesus was born of the Virgin Mary and conceived by the Holy Spirit, not by a mortal man;
3) Jesus was sinless, crucified, and resurrected from the grave;
4) We all face God on judgment day and Jesus will take his followers with him to heaven;
5) The Bible is God's written word to us.

A few outward or visible clues that a person is Christian may include:

1) Repentance—a changed, more Christ-like life including patience, humility, kindness,

selflessness, and a more loving person; possibly different friends;

2) Routine prayer; reading and studying God's word;

3) A desire to worship with other Christians;

4) Defending Christ, the Bible, and fellow Christians.

Conversely, there are also discernable clues leading one to think someone is not a Christian. Although this is not an all-inclusive list, here are a few:

1) Personal rejection or ridicule of Christ or the Bible;

2) The display of hostility towards Christians or their beliefs;

3) A desire to remove God or Christianity from the public arena;

4) An indifference or apathy towards God and Christianity.

This last group contains a sizeable number of people and deserves more discussion. These may be "good" people—solid citizens who would make good friends. They live on your block, you work with them, they are on your softball team, they don't cheat on their taxes, they don't drink or smoke, they never curse, they volunteer at homeless shelters, they help little old ladies cross the street, they may even go to church regularly and believe in God.

This group is filled with people of sound moral character. Surely these people are going to be in heaven aren't they? After all, they believe in God—isn't that all that is necessary?

Quite frankly, that's not enough.

Reading that is like running into a brick wall for many people. I hope you finish the book! It's the kind of statement that gets Christians labeled as judgmental and intolerant. A mature Christian realizes that many people think their eternity is secure simply because they believe in God. The Bible says there will be many who thought they would be in heaven but Christ will say "I never knew you" (**Matthew 7:21–23**). Christians don't want others left out of heaven. We want as many as possible in heaven.

Christians are commanded to love everyone, including non-Christians. Christians have family members and friends who are not saved. We care about their eternity too. If you love someone, and believe in a judgment day, wouldn't you want them to be prepared? No Christian wants to see anyone banished to hell for an eternity.

It is important enough to repeat—simply believing there is a God isn't going to punch your ticket into heaven. Remember, the angel Lucifer—Satan, was created by God. Satan has been in the presence of God. Satan believes God exists. Satan *knows* God exists. Satan, who believes in God, will not be in heaven. Let that sink in.

WHAT DO I DO NEXT?

This book is not intended to be a scare tactic. A person can't be frightened to a faith in God by threatening them with hell. As a Christian for forty years, I tell you these things because: 1) they are true as recorded in the Bible; 2) they are unpopular; 3) they are being shouted down; and 4) they are intentionally being hidden from you by people (hostile to Christianity) in positions of power and influence in our culture. These people are in national government, political parties, Hollywood, higher education, the media, and unfortunately, many churches.

You will be able to develop a relationship with God once you realize that the feelings of emptiness, hopelessness, or not knowing your purpose in life originate from a heart without God. There is an empty space in your heart that only God can fill. A new job, different spouse, bigger house, nicer car, more alcohol, or world travel is not going to fill that space.

Only God fits that space. He placed that space there and is knocking at the door of your heart but you have to open the door (**Revelation 3:20**). He won't force himself on you.

You have read this book, what should you do next?

Firstly, you should not panic—you aren't in this alone. There are seven billion people in this world and most of them aren't Christian.

Secondly, there *are* many, many Christians in this world who know people like you exist and we want to help. The Christians in your immediate world can serve as a source of encouragement, help you find Christian guidance and answer many of your questions. Surround yourself with good Christian friends who are concerned for your spiritual welfare.

Thirdly, you will need to find a good church. Many churches have strayed from the Gospel—the teachings of Christ. Sadly, many of their members don't even recognize that because they haven't studied their Bibles enough to recognize the bad doctrine coming from the pulpit. These churches are harming people spiritually and are not worthy to be called Christian churches. Hopefully, your Christian friends will know a "Gospel preachin' Bible-believin'" church.

Fourthly, be aware that Christian radio and television exist. There are some fantastic Gospel-based ministries available to you in the privacy of your home or on the way to work. That daily commute to work could be used to learn more about Christ and build up your spiritual muscle.

Finally, stay interested in your desire to develop and nurture a faith in Christ. It's not easy to begin a Christian faith in this world hostile to Christian values. It could cost you some friends, a job, or a position of influence. It may be a radically different lifestyle from the way you are living now; but *don't give up*. God will not give up on you because he created you, he loves you, and he desperately wants a relationship with you.

Once you decide to follow Jesus, your spiritual growth begins. You will continue to mature with Bible study, prayer, and fellowship with Christians. A feeling of hope will appear, leading you to approach life's challenges differently. Along the way, you (and others) will notice that you are a different person. They will see you as a more forgiving, kind, caring, gentle, and loving person. You will develop a joy and confidence leading you to share your faith with others. Feelings of contentment will develop because you have discovered the reason for your existence.

These things will happen because you will have become a person who knows, without a doubt, that your eternity will be spent with Jesus. You will be a person—who has become a Christian.

ABOUT THE AUTHOR

Dr. Greg Gillham was born in Scotia, Nebraska. He grew up fishing, hunting, and playing baseball. After completing his Bachelor of Science degree at University of Nebraska in Lincoln, he attended medical school and completed his internal medicine residency at the University of Nebraska Medical Center. He has been a hospitalist since 1999. He and his wife have four horses and a beagle. Flower gardening is a hobby he enjoys along with NFL football.

CPSIA information can be obtained
at www.ICGtesting.com
Printed in the USA
FFHW020128251019
55717206-61586FF